The Non-Boring
Vacation Packing
Guide

More Non-Boring Travel Guides

**The Non-Boring Safe Travel Guide:
Save Your Back, Time, and Money**

**The Non-Boring Travel Money Guide:
Dollars, Rupiah, and Sense**
(coming soon)

The Non-Boring Vacation Packing Guide

Save Your Back, Time, and Money

ELISABETH SOWERBUTTS

www.NonBoringTravelGuides.com

First Print Edition September, 2012

Also available as an eBook

ISBN:978-1479303274

Published by *Non-Boring Travel Guides*
www.nonBoringTravelGuides.com

Disclaimer

This book contains information regarding travel that is the author's own opinions and experiences. It is published for general reference, entertainment and travel dreaming purposes only and is not intended to be a substitute for independent financial advice, medical advice or any other type of advice offered by the relevant professional. The author disclaims any personal liability, for the information contained within.

If you have specific issues, seek qualified advice. Preferably from someone who spent years in school learning this stuff, the author did not.

The author has made every effort to ensure the accuracy and completeness of the information contained within, she assumes no responsibility for errors, inaccuracies, omissions or inconsistencies.

CONTENTS

Introduction: Or Why A Book About Packing?   9

PART 1: Packing - A Travel Philosophy   17

So Why Do We Over Pack?   21

Why Less is More   27

When Light is Not Enough   30

Key Points - The WHY of Packing Light   34

PART 2: What Stuff to Pack   35

Work out the Stuff That Matters   36

Stuff to Wear   50

Gear to Wear in the Heat   58

Gear to Wear in the Cold   65

eStuff – Do You Need It?   70

Key Points: The WHAT of Packing   76

PART 3: Packing Lists, Tips and Tricks 77

Security is (Mostly) In Your Mind 81

A Short List of Useful Travel Gear 86

A Longer List of Useless Travel Gear 89

Key Points: Tips and Tricks 95

PART 4:Luggage and How to Pack It 97

The Debate: Rigid Case or Backpack? 98

How to Pack 103

Carry It On? Maybe, Maybe Not 106

Key Points Luggage Packing 110

About The Author 111

Sign Up For A Free Travel Newsletter 112

WHY A BOOK ABOUT PACKING?

It was the night before my first real solo trip. I had tried to get everything into my pack several times, but it just wouldn't all fit. Time was running out. The day before departure, it was too late to buy another, bigger bag, and frankly this one was already as large a bag as I could carry.

"Okay," said my more experienced friend, "take everything out and lay it out on the bed."

I followed her instructions, and she then took half of the items away. "Take what's left," she insisted.

I argued for the black strapless ball gown – it didn't need ironing and I loved it and I hadn't even worn it yet! What if I got invited to a real fancy night out and I had nothing to wear?

"Leave it here," she said, "I'll mail it to you if you need it."

She removed five of my eight t-shirts. But, hey, I was planning on being away for a year – I needed lots of t-shirts! She then said a truly wonderful thing, advice I hadn't found in my "How to Travel the World for $10/Day" guidebook (well, yes, it was a couple of decades ago).

She offered, "If you need it that much, you can buy it there!"

Seriously, the world has shops? Who'd have guessed? That planned one-year trip turned into three, and eventually I returned to her place. She gave me back my still unworn dress, which was now out of fashion and had mysteriously shrunk in storage. I ended up giving it to a charity shop, with gratitude for a lesson well learned.

You are looking for a vacation packing list, but what I'm going to give you is a packing philosophy. Basically, I travel with a carry-on sized bag which is light enough to indeed carry on. If I'm traveling on a small aircraft with limited overhead space, I may have to check the bag, but it's not because I've over-packed.

I started traveling light because I had no option. With no money for porters and taxis, I had to carry my luggage myself and I wasn't very fit. My bag had to be light. Now I travel light by choice. Why? It's simply a better travel experience. And, that's the point of this book: to explain to you why it's important to carry just enough, but no more – and to give you the tools to create your own vacation packing list. You really can pack light, and save your back, time and money when you travel.

I have read book after book about traveling. I love to travel, but I can't always afford to. In between travels, I would devour both guidebooks of places I hadn't been to yet and various "how to" guides -- how to pack, how to get a good deal in the Caribbean, etc. Perhaps you've done the same?

Some of those books were good, but most were average. Frankly, I've never found a good packing book. I've read books on how to pack for business, how to rearrange a scarf 25 different ways to personalize your outfits, how to pack for women, how to pack for children – you name it. Most of those books didn't reflect what I'd learned about packing, wisdom I'd gleaned by actually doing it, a lot.

This might be heresy given the title of this book, but I believe that definitive packing lists are nonsense. You can't define a useful list for someone else and most generic lists focus on clothing, the most personal and most easily purchased part of your load. Some of the recommendations are just plain silly, too. Why, for example, would you need a bottle for water in countries that sell bottled water on every street corner and several places in between?

I've traveled for over 30 years. I've traveled for work and for fun. I've traveled on expense accounts and I've paid my own way. I've traveled solo and as a couple. I've occasionally joined group tours. I've packed for climates that varied from heavy snow in Europe to the baking Australian outback. I've packed for tropical islands and for temperate mountain ranges. I haven't yet packed for Antarctica, but I've packed for every other continent.

In this book I hope to share with you not just what works for packing but what doesn't and to demonstrate how you can develop your own personal packing style. Whether you are packing for a two-week family vacation or that once-in-a-lifetime trip around the world, I hope to show you how a well-designed approach to packing really will improve your vacation, make it easier and more fun and save you money on luggage transport charges.

As a side benefit, these small changes in behavior may even help save the planet. Think of all the airline fuel NOT burned to get your 66 pounds of "necessities" around the world!

I suppose if you really don't need to budget for your travel, then you don't need this book. You can simply hire an extra taxi for the gear and leave the packing to the maid and/or the nanny. In that case, this book is not for you, but you probably assumed that when you saw the price tag!

I am not a poor backpacker any more. I can afford to stay in 5-star properties (in Vietnam, at least, during the off-season), but I still like to travel rather than just follow the crowd. I will quite happily book a fancy hotel deal and, upon check-out, walk the half mile to the road to flag down the local bus rather than pay $80 for the hotel's luxury car transfer to the airport. Ultimately, this saves me about $77, and I tend to go with that option for two reasons:

The first has to do with my attitude. I am supremely confident there will be a bus and it will stop, at least in the third world. (Interestingly, I might be less inclined to risk this in some U.S. cities).

The second is the key: I have bags I can carry myself without effort.

Even if your budget and inclination allow for the more expensive airport transfer, there is always that time when the proverbial can and does hit the fan.

For us it happened in Greece, upon arriving back on Rhodes from a side trip to another nearby island. Instead of arriving at Rhodes' busy port in the center of town, the boat we were on docked at some unpronounceable spot some 20 miles (30km) away from the center of town. There were no taxis milling about and no buses because it was a Sunday/a holiday/a strike or some-such. (My Greek wasn't up to the fine detail.)

Instead of panicking, we simply shrugged and walked up to the main road some 10 minutes away. A warm early morning, it was obvious the day was only going to get hotter. We waited for a half hour and first got a lift in the back of a pickup and second in a tiny mini. Be assured: the mini wouldn't have worked for us if our luggage didn't fit on our laps.

Now, I don't routinely hitchhike and it was my partner's first time (it's a potentially dangerous way to see the world and unpredictable, too), but when you are stuck on the wrong side of Rhodes with no town in sight, not much water and no food on a hot Sunday, it's a pretty good option to have in your back pocket. And, quite often, that option only exists if you have minimal luggage!

Whether I choose to carry on or check it, I can travel indefinitely with a carry-on sized bag that weighs 15-17lb (7-8kg), plus a small day bag. (Did I mention that I work when I travel so I need to take a laptop with me?) If the journey requires closed-toe, sturdy shoes, I will need to wear those; otherwise, everything I need fits in my carry-on.

That combo goes places where large luggage can't. It will fit on my lap, if necessary. It will fit under the seat or in the overhead rack on a bus not equipped for luggage storage. It can be placed on a rack above a train seat without risking injury to my shoulder or back, and it will typically fit in a small locker at the station so as to avoid a more expensive luggage storage option, if need be. Most importantly, it means I can walk almost as far with it as I can without it.

I've never met anyone who wished they had brought more stuff with them on a trip, but I've met plenty of people who envy my small, light load. Most people who travel repeatedly learn through bitter experience that less really is more when packing. The point of this book is to eliminate – or at least minimize – that learning curve for you. (Speaking of learning curves, be sure to double check the port location and bus schedules if your journey includes arriving on Rhodes from the cute little island of Halki!)

I hope this book is the last one you'll need to buy on vacation packing. It's written with the aim of teaching you how to pack for a vacation which will save your back, your time and your money.

Elisabeth Sowerbutts

Wellington, N.Z.

September 2012

PART 1: PACKING - A TRAVEL PHILOSOPHY

Most books of this type will begin by explaining why you do or do not need a new set of matching wheeled luggage and/or arguing the merits of a soft bag v. a hard-shell suitcase. We will get to that, but let's start with the important thing in this process: why you need to think quite carefully about your packing list.

My philosophy of packing is quite simple: less is more. Take what you need but no more. The trick, of course, is defining what you "need" with specificity.

Packing light isn't just a matter of saving your back or saving some airline luggage fees; those are really just added benefits. Packing light is truly at the essence of how to make whatever type of trip you are taking more enjoyable. Why? Travel is all about experience, and packing light improves the experience.

The 20-somethings sitting on the Thai beach chatting to friends on Facebook on their iPhone are missing the moment – missing that they are at this very moment on a stunning beach in a fascinating country surrounded by some of the nicest people on the planet and totally oblivious to both the annoying beach vendor trying to sell them a tacky snow-dome of Patong Beach for 20 baht, the majestic sunset and the local families swimming fully-clothed.

Similarly, travelers who must relentlessly track and count their multiple suitcases and other bags as they enter and exit taxis and hotel receptions are giving too much attention to their luggage and missing at least a portion of the life and fun going on around them. At best, they are wasting time and effort which could be more pleasantly deployed – sampling the local beer in a pub, perhaps – and at worst, they are ruining their honeymoon dream trip because they're worried about whether they've lost the cream-colored bag with the six pairs of shoes in it.

Now just to be clear: it's obvious I now prefer to travel light, but I haven't always had that luxury. I have experienced the alternative, tracking and counting seven bags shared between two adults as we schlepped between planes, buses and taxis. I've combined work with travel when I've had to carry a large case filled with a computer (yes, a computer, not a laptop), books, papers and cables. My personal record for weight carried without paying extra airline fees was 97lbs (44kg), checked between two of us, and each with a carry-on bag weighing about 22lbs (10kg).

It wasn't fun. It was stressful remembering how many bags I needed to track and checking to ensure I had them. Loading and unloading those bags was hard on my back and my arms, and it was hard on my budget when door-to-door taxis were required because I couldn't walk even short distances or manage the airport bus. I did it because I had to, not because I wanted to.

Perhaps you think you can't travel light, reasoning: I'm older, I need to look good at the opera, I'm traveling for months from the snow to a tropical beach, etc. Then again, perhaps you've just made some of the best arguments of all for traveling with less instead of more!

Older people are, in general, less fit than their younger counterparts. They may indeed be traveling with medical conditions that require medication, but even a complicated cocktail of pharmaceuticals won't require much weight (or space, if it's packed right). Your age has no relevance to the rest of your packing list.

I personally love the opera and going to a ballet performance at Covent Garden's famous theater was a personal highlight of a London visit. It didn't require me to pack a tiara, travel iron and full-length evening dress, however. I wore black dressy slacks, a pretty silk blouse that weighted next to nothing and a less than sophisticated but quite waterproof (and quickly removed and checked) jacket. Sure, I didn't have a handbag or makeup, but no one threw me out or even looked at me twice because of it. And, the ballet performance – the experience – remains a cherished memory I can carry with me for all of my days.

Traveling for six months needs more gear than traveling for a six-day vacation, right? Actually, no; quite the opposite, in fact!

When I first backpacked through Asia, I took a "small" 3660 cu in (60 L) backpack, the bottom third of which was consumed by one full-sized fluffy towel and a large sleeping bag. Even if I carried a towel and a sleeping bag on my current travels (which I don't), I'd still only need a 2440 cu in (40 L) pack because, with technological improvements, those two items now require much less space. If your travels require it, an ultra-compact (but still warm) sleeping bag and a super-absorbent towel (the size of a tea towel) are two travel items well worth purchasing, but we'll cover that in more detail soon.

In this chapter, I want to explain the WHY behind taking less than you think you need on your next vacation.

SO, WHY DO WE OVER PACK?

Even experienced travelers struggle with packing. Beginners don't know where to start, and the default human instinct is to take everything, just in case. After all, Dr. Livingstone exploring Africa or the early American pioneers didn't travel light, right? Their expeditions literally took the kitchen sink! But, then again, we aren't packing for an exploration into unknown lands, are we? We're packing for a vacation. Our goal should be to keep it simple and make it fun!

If you are planning a self-supported expedition to Africa or anywhere else, this book may not be the best one for you. For the rest of you, though, I'm going to try to explain and encourage you to adopt the wisdom of that amazing travel secret my friend shared with me so many years ago.

Understand: you are not going to the ends of civilization, and you do not need to be self-supporting. The world is literally chock-full of places where you can buy stuff – malls, shops, stalls, markets, etc. If you run out of shampoo, I am 99.9% confident you will be able to buy it.

Over the years I've traveled, it's become easier and easier to buy whatever I need on the road. Globalization is my friend and yours, too! Not only can you buy shampoo virtually anywhere, you may very well find your preferred brand albeit labeled in an unfamiliar script or language.

Even still, I see an increasing number of tourists carrying increasingly large and heavy bags in the face of increasingly restrictive airline rules. Why? Two reasons, I think:

- the perception that the world is a dangerous place (thanks to the mass media); and
- the marketing of travel gear.

Fear of the 'Dangerous' World

Every time I have a conversation about this with a supposedly rational and intelligent person who follows the news, I get the same response: it's different now, the world is more dangerous, you have to be more careful, etc. From my observations, post-9/11 Americans are the world citizens most susceptible to this fear.

By any rational measure, however, the world has become safer for travelers over the last 30 years. Look at Europe: last century the continent was a no-go zone as "world war" broke out over its entirety, not once but twice. As recently as the 1990s, the Balkans was a dangerous war-zone, off limits to visitors. For nearly 50 years the Eastern part of the continent was so cut-off from the West that not only could these countries' own people not leave, outside tourism was strongly discouraged.

Today, on the other hand, even formerly isolationist Albania welcomes the dollars tourists bring with them. There hasn't been a nuclear bomb since 1945. Even the "Arab Spring" which swept North Africa from Tunisia to Syria in early 2011, although not without casualties, caused little more than a brief and slight inconvenience to the area's visitors.

I have a friend who was traveling in Syria in April 2011, at the same time the world's media reported riots in the streets and shootings in Damascus and Homs. She and her husband peacefully traversed the whole country without danger, fear or disruption. They experienced welcoming people, stunning scenery, crumbling ruins and excellent food. They didn't require a car, a driver or security; they relied solely on local transport. They didn't speak or read Arabic. They were just fine.

In February 2011, Christchurch, New Zealand was rocked by a 6.3-magnitude earthquake. Nearly 200 people died, and the city's central business district was decimated, with over 200 buildings destroyed or subsequently demolished. The airport was closed for a few hours, but there was never any problem with tourists staying near the airport or at nearby Akaroa, nor was it difficult for them to catch a bus anywhere else in the South Island or rent a car in which to travel independently. Indeed, the central city tour and the Anglican Cathedral are closed for the foreseeable future, but there was really no reason for travelers to cancel a planned trip. Sadly, however, many did because the media focused on the relatively limited damage and failed to present the whole picture. The local tourist industry suffered more from this unbalanced impression of the state of the city in the media, than from the actual earthquake.

The media's motivation and ability to bring us every protest and every natural disaster – and in high definition color and surround sound, of course – does not help us acquire and enjoy a balanced view of the world's dangers.

At least at a subconscious level, we fear the world and fear the unknown. Even if that's not our instinct, we are bound to experience this on some level as we consider our nearest-and-dearest's well-intentioned warnings about how a planned vacation to Thailand will likely see us locked up for life as drug smugglers, sold to white slave traders or robbed of our last credit card.

The reality is a little more prosaic. Yes, tourists die in Thailand each year; typically they die riding motorbikes (for which they often have no experience or training) and driving on the "wrong" side of the road or on roads they are unfamiliar with. Some die from drinking copious amounts of alcohol, particularly young visitors who may never have previously consumed alcohol in their lives. You can certainly die in Thailand, just as you can die in your home town.

The underlying psychology is quite simple: traveling is equated with danger, at least in our subconscious minds, and most of our friends and relatives will constantly remind us of this if we dare to book a vacation to a "well-known risky location" (i.e., away from home).

Therefore, in an attempt to quell our impending doom, we over pack, "just to be on the safe side," you know? Familiar "things" provide comfort, so if we bring more of them with us we'll be safer, won't we? If we come equipped with the portable safe, the personal alarm and the pepper spray, we'll be okay, right?

The Clever Marketing of Travel Gear

It used to be that if you wanted a water bottle you bought a bottle of water once and reused it. Now you can buy a collapsible, foldaway version and take it with you. It used to be that if you were concerned about a bag being snatched while you slept on a train you bought a length of goat chain locally and a lock. These days, if you believe the marketing, you need a Pacsafe (tm) and possibly a pack alarm, as well, if you expect to arrive at your destination with your bag.

Where we once kept dirty clothes in a random plastic bag and replaced it as it was lost along the way, now we need a custom, light-weight, breathable, organic, green laundry bag, available in three sizes, for your convenience. At least that's what the marketing department would have us believe.

Now don't get me wrong: I own and enjoy some travel gadgets. Honestly, though, I don't require many, and most of the ones I do own I've had for a decade or more. No travel gear manufacturer has made fat profits off me. But, indeed, they could have once, before I started traveling seriously. When I was a planning my travels, I was a sucker for guidebooks and I would have been a sucker for that oh-so-cute set of expanding plates. No doubt I might have eyed the travelers' toiletries bag with detachable first aid kit, as well.

Marketing has bombarded the would-be vacationer with messages suggesting they can't leave home without a customized and organic set of packing solutions to fit in their coordinated carrying solution. Oddly, though, some of us oldies manage to get by just fine with a manageable bag and a "set" of smaller bags we picked up free on our last shopping trip.

I can say with confidence: you'll be much better off taking the money you save while avoiding the more-is-better school of travel gadgets and investing it in a well-made bag that will last you for many years and many travels to come.

WHY LESS IS MORE

So, why travel light anyway? What's wrong with taking a few extra items, just in case? Won't they make my trip more enjoyable and comfortable? In a word, no. In fact, those few extra items are far more likely to create stress.

The subtitle for this book – "pack the low stress way: saving your back, time and money" – isn't a marketing slogan. It's what I've actually seen and experienced. I live in a town frequented by young backpackers, in a country that offers superb hosteling facilities. I regularly see six-foot young men dwarfed by and struggling under the weight of their packs. While they may end up pretty fit from the experience, I do wonder if they'll later develop and suffer stress-related injuries from it!

Older people are just as bad, albeit often not as obviously. Invariably, they are never seen in public with their luggage, but that's because they require door-to-door transfers to deal with all their many and large suitcases. Frankly, if I could afford door-to-door transfers, I'd rather spend the money on a spa day or a better bottle of wine.

Apart from the transfers, you may also end up paying extra for a pack that takes up a seat in a shared taxi or shuttle mini-van. Even if you don't pay more in dollars, you will experience the extra level of hassle involved with securing or checking bags into the luggage compartments of the trains, planes, boats and buses on which you travel.

Transporting and stowing larger bags obviously costs more because a) you have to; and b) you may well pay per item at a luggage check or pay more for a larger-sized locker. (Not to mention how returning to collect your bag before you go on your way often presents an additional, unnecessary hassle.) Planes are the obvious place where you will save serious money traveling without checked luggage. As you're no doubt aware, most airlines these days charge for anything that needs to be checked.

And, it's not just the physical struggle of carrying large amounts of luggage. It's the repacking. If there's one part of travel I dislike (along with long-haul flights in cattle class), it's packing and re-packing. Trying to fit all your stuff back in the bag it arrived in and making sure you didn't miss anything can be psychologically exhausting. If you have three shirts with you (and assuming you are wearing one of them), there are only two to pack. On the other hand, if you have a week's worth of shirts with you, there are six shirts to account for and pack. If you have only two to pack you are quite apt to notice if you're missing one (50% of your shirts), whereas with six shirts, one can easily go AWOL and hang forever, overlooked and abandoned on the back of the bathroom door.

The frugality movement has become popular in the U.S. in recent years, and there have been many millions of words written on the liberation that de-cluttering your life can bring as you down-size your possessions and maybe your home. Learning how to pack light is a good way to start enjoying this sense of freedom!

WHEN LIGHT IS NOT ENOUGH

Once, and it was only once, I became engaged in an online argument with someone who, in my opinion, wanted to travel too light. His aim was to travel without a bag at all – with all his gear stored in his pockets! That is the single exception, though, and most people do over-pack.

Interestingly, though, even those who carry too much may not carry the right things. From my experience, those folks are the ones most apt to forget to bring some key personal, difficult-to-replace items which would have improved their trip.

I've met the odd person who's traveling unhappily because they can't take what they consider to be good photos. For many of us, a pocket-sized, point-and-shoot digital camera is entirely sufficient. However, the keen amateur photographer who left the good camera at home – fearing its theft or damage – who now finds him/herself surrounded by exotic and spectacular scenery may be absolutely miserable with the inability to indulge their hobby. If your hobby requires gear and you will be miserable without it, then bring it – be it camera gear, a watercolor painting kit or crossword puzzle books. It's important to take note of how our hobbies and creative outlets are often quite important to our well-being, at home and as we travel.

Other people are just plain annoying. They never seem to have nail scissors, a needle and thread with which to sew a button on, sanitary products or the like, no matter how many suitcases they are willing to lug around. (Oddly, travelers who lack these basic items are usually the same ones who have a different outfit for every day of the week, along with matching accoutrements and a travel hairdryer. Go figure.) These folks aren't just traveling with too much stuff, they are neglecting the necessities that really matter. Frankly, none of these things take much space – and you really can't substitute anything else for them – so do bring them along.

Personally, I don't carry an extensive first aid kit. I don't know how to construct my own plaster cast or strap a strained shoulder, even at home, so I don't bother taking the items I might need to do those things with me when traveling. On the other hand, I always have Tylenol, motion sickness pills and a re-hydration mixture, and that's because I know there's a good chance I'll need them at some point during my travels. I also know that when I do need them will coincide directly with when I won't feel at all like walking the streets looking for a pharmacy.

Although there's no real valid argument against trying to pack light, admittedly it's sometimes difficult to achieve. My partner needs to carry a tail suit when we travel to compete in a dance competition and that makes for an extra heavy bag on those trips. Most of the time, though, people carry far more than they need purely out of either laziness – not thinking through what they'll actually need and use – or fear. In an avoidance of considered, rational planning, they pack a variety of outfits to wear for an array of contingencies, most of which probably won't happen.

Be brave, go light. Be green, go light. Be minimalist, go light.

Go light and save money for the fun stuff.

Get closer to the locals, have more fun, save your back.

Go light.

I hope I've convinced you that if we can get past our fears – so often exacerbated by large doses of TV news – the world isn't really all that dangerous and moving around in it requires much less "armor" than we might imagine, even when we are far from home. There's no need to over-pack to alleviate concern about circumstances and events that will probably never happen.

I hope you see the folly in the delusion, against all evidence, that convinces us there will be no shops where we are going. Ironically, we will assign time to shop for souvenirs (which will probably end up gathering dust in someone's closet), but we freely forfeit the fun and education of finding the right size shirt in a night market or working out which shampoo to buy at a local store.

So, after a brief recap of this chapter's key points, let's take a look at what you should take with you on your vacation.

KEY POINTS - THE WHY OF PACKING LIGHT

- Taking less minimizes stress and therefore maximizes enjoyment of your vacation. You're not "getting away" so you can be more stressed, are you?
- Driven by an inflated fear of what may happen and the allure of cute travel gadgets, we often take too much stuff on our travels.
- Almost anyone can learn to pack light, and it's a particularly useful skill for the older and the less fit among us. Most frequent and experienced business travelers have learned to pack light, and so can you.
- Take fewer clothes, but make sure you have essential, non-clothing items you may need in a hurry. Everything else can be bought, if and when the need arises.

PART 2: WHAT STUFF TO PACK

Hopefully I have convinced you that you can easily minimize what you take with you when you travel and that there are substantial benefits to be realized from doing so. This naturally begs the question: so, what the heck should I take? Well, since I am not you, I don't exactly know. I can, however, provide some suggestions and useful questions to ask yourself to help you develop your own personal, perfect packing list.

In this section we will look at WHAT is and is not important to pack and also cover how to travel without carrying a pile of dirty laundry with you.

WORK OUT THE STUFF THAT MATTERS

If you dozed through psychology class you may vaguely remember a gentleman named Maslow and his "hierarchy of needs." To summarize briefly, Maslow's hierarchy asserts we know instinctively our basic health or safety are far more important than fitting into a social situation, finding a mate or choosing the right type of interior furnishings.

Maslow explained – albeit indirectly – why worrying about whether to take three blue and two red bras or just six white ones is far less important than considering how you will access your travel funds on the road or whether you will have an ample supply of an important prescription medication.

Maslow would likely counsel travelers the most important items on a packing list are:

- Documents;

- Money (and/or today's equivalent, plastic cards); and
- Anything that's vitally important for your health.

Unfortunately, in today's world you can't go far without documentation. Simply crossing the border from the U.S. into Mexico or Canada requires a passport, and even if you are just traveling locally, you will need identification.

Further afield, a passport has always been essential, and many countries require that your passport remain valid for at least six months AFTER your departure. Be sure to check your country's restrictions and your passport's expiration date before you get too far involved in planning your great adventure or vacation.

Also, be aware that losing your passport is a MAJOR hassle. Avoid this at all costs. We'll talk more about how to protect your passport later on, but for now just note you should also have access to a copy of your passport. A photocopy will do, but you can also take a photo of the main data page to leave on your camera's memory card and/or send the image to an email account you can access from any Internet cafe.

Although I rarely carry much cash on me at home, on vacation I will often have a few hundred dollars of the local currency or US$. When the power goes down, ATMs and EFTPOS machines don't work. When your card has been frozen by the bank because you don't normally buy mojitos in Anguilla, cash is a very good thing to have on hand. (Before you leave home, it's a good idea to let each of your card providers know you may be indulging in a somewhat unusual spending pattern so they don't suspect fraud and complicate your trip.) I also carry at least two debit or credit cards, preferably associated with different banks or at least different accounts, so if one card is lost and the account needs to be frozen the other one will still work.

When we talk about items essential for your health and safety, please remember I'm not talking about a personal alarm or pepper spray (which is illegal in most countries, incidentally). Instead, I mean any medicine you need to take on a regular basis. If you're traveling with a companion, then split your supplies between the two bags so if the worst happens to one you still have some of this essential medication. You should also carry at least a small supply in another place you can easily access, like your day bag. Take a copy of the written prescription, too, again either in photocopy or digital form. While you might not need the actual document in much of the world, it can provide the world-recognized, technical language necessary to enable a pharmacy to sell you what you need. If you have serious allergies and need an EpiPen, make sure you have it with you along with a doctor's note explaining your requirements (for curious airport security employees' sake).

If you can't see without glasses, make sure you have a spare pair. (I usually carry a pair of prescription sunglasses as my back up.) If you are traveling to a location with lower medical costs than your own country, Asia for example, you may prefer to have a spare pair made when you arrive, instead. It's also a good idea to stash a copy of your vision prescription with your other photocopied or digitally saved important documents.

Although you can buy almost anything anywhere in the world, there is a short list of items that can be difficult to find outside of the Western world:

- Shoes in large sizes can present a problem. Although you can almost always have large-sized clothing custom made, this isn't so easy with shoes. If you have large feet and need shoes in Asia, you may be in trouble. In a pinch, women may find men's shoes to suffice. I had to go to the big-and-tall men's shop in Bangkok once to find thongs to fit, and I'm only a 44 wide!
- You will encounter a similar problem finding bras with bigger than a D cup. While it's possible to get a made-to-measure bra in some places, most tailors are male so this option is less than ideal.

Of course you will need a few more items than those discussed above, but those are the vitally important ones. Everything else you can buy along the way!

So, What Stuff Do You Need to Pack?

Before we get into the inventory of what you'll need, let's talk briefly about what you shouldn't take with you. Don't take anything that's valuable, particularly anything of sentimental value. If your mother's gold chain is important to you because it once belonged to her, the few hundred dollars payout from your travel insurance policy will hardly compensate for losing it on vacation and will likely lead to an unpleasant travel memory.

Likewise, don't take anything irreplaceable. If you have your entire business on your laptop including all your client details and accounting balances, don't take it until – at the very least – you have a full and current backup in a very safe place. Make sure you have a backup of any software you use on the laptop, too.

Documents

In addition to your passport, there are few more pieces of paper you may need. If you have travel insurance – and I believe that's often a good idea – take a copy of your policy number and also the insurance company's assistance phone number. Again, a photocopy works, but a digital copy in your email account can usually be accessed easily in an emergency. Some insurance companies provide a small card to take with you and instruct that you can leave the rest of the paperwork at home; take the card, if so instructed.

If you are driving overseas, you may need an International Driver's License. They are inexpensive and easy to get at your local automobile association. It's basically a multi-lingual translation of your local license, which you will need to carry with you, as well.

Reservations and "proof of onward travel" is an interesting one. The irony of the demise of the travel agent and the growth of online bookings is that I now carry more paper than ever before. Checking in online is now the norm for many airlines, and you will need to get a paper print out of your boarding pass in most cases. (Some airlines now allow paperless check-in using a special, QR, barcode on your smartphone.) Governments, however, haven't caught up with technology (how surprising!), and most want "hard copy" (i.e., paper) proof of onward travel and not just an image on your phone or laptop. Hotels you have prepaid in advance may also insist on a paper receipt, although they are far more likely to have a printer handy to assist you than a border control agent. I use a plastic, water-resistant folder to hold all the travel reservations paperwork I need to take with me.

If you have spare passport photos, take those with you, too. While these will often stay unused in your folder from trip to trip, sometimes they will save you time and hassle if a photo is necessary for some sort of documentation. This tip came in handy for me when I arrived in Cambodia, where visitors needed a photo to complete the on-arrival visa process. And, apart from visas, these photos can come in handy for theme park or transport passes, fishing or diving licenses, etc.

First Aid Kit and Sewing Kit

Generally speaking, anywhere with a tourist industry offers local medical services, and you should only carry the medical gear you know how to use. I travel very light in this regard, but if I had some medical training, I might carry more than I do. I carry these basics in a very small pouch:

- some bandages in various sizes;
- small tweezers (for removing splinters); and
- small nail scissors (for various needs, including cutting tape and trimming blisters).

If I am worried about blisters, I'll carry special blister bandages in my assortment, and I do also carry something for headaches and motion sickness. I don't carry liquids (for obvious reasons) or throat lozenges (they melt quite easily). I've never found any effective food-poisoning medicine, but I do carry oral rehydration powder packets in case I eat something dodgy. These do work, and they can also be useful if you're feeling ill because you've been out in the hot sun for too long.

If you wear contacts, you will need to carry a small bottle of cleaning solution. This is not available everywhere, but you should be able to find it in larger towns and resorts.

Travel is very rough on your clothes, so I do carry thread and a needle for emergency repairs. The needle, if sterilized in a flame, can also be useful for removing a splinter. If I have clothing with a spare button, I sew it onto an inside seam before I leave home so, if needed, it's easier to find.

I usually carry sunscreen and insect repellent, as my skin is fair and seems to act as an attractant to mosquitoes. I take the strongest (30%) DEET-based insect repellent I can find. (If you are staying at the same hotel as me you probably won't need any repellant!) It smells and it's not nice to plastic, but it works. While you can find both insect repellent and sunscreen almost everywhere the sun shines, you will often pay more for it at tourist destinations – sometimes a lot more if you're going straight to a remote island or resort. You may want to bring some with you and then abandon it upon your return and use the space it required for your homeward-bound souvenirs.

By the way, regarding "natural" insect repellants – they work, but only on people unlikely to be bitten anyway. Some people have the right blood chemistry and don't get many bites (my partner is one). Test after scientific test has proven DEET's efficacy over any natural insect deterrent, and dengue and malaria are serious diseases which kill thousands each year. Needless to say, mosquito bites are best avoided. While I have yet to see any scientific evidence suggesting any danger in using DEET, the chemical does some real damage to plastic. Be careful of using it around your laptop or phone if you want the keys to still have characters on them.

If I am staying in an accommodation without air conditioning – which often means open windows and mosquito nets – I will buy mosquito coils and a lighter for a few cents soon after I arrive. Don't try to bring these items with you, though. You should never try to get on a plane with a cigarette lighter, and the coils are fragile and break easily. Besides, you can easily buy them in any part of the world that has a mosquito problem.

Security Stuff

I pack my common sense, but not my paranoia. Basically, I don't want to spend a vacation worrying about stuff I might damage or lose. If I care about stuff, it stays at home. While losing your suitcase is a nuisance, losing your passport, money and/or cards could be a game-over show-stopper. I am with my money and cards at all times, 24/7.

If I'm staying somewhere upmarket, I may use the room safe, but frankly most of these safes seem more a danger to me than a protection. Usually I just carry my important items on my body using a "money belt" (I don't like belts, though, and find the shoulder-holster style far more comfortable). If I'm going to be spending the day by the pool, I will usually lock my important things in the bottom of a decrepit and grubby main bag. I also always travel with a good quality combination lock (so I can't lose the keys) to secure my bag's zipper.

Seriously, don't take items like pepper spray; it's illegal on aircraft and in many countries. If you are American, you already live in one of the most dangerous countries in the world. Outside of some war zones and failed states, the risk of being robbed at gun or knife point is very, very low – much lower than in many major American cities. Developing countries have lots of thieves, but they won't threaten you face on. I've lost valuables twice, and both times it was while my attention was elsewhere making me vulnerable to the pick pocket or sneak thief.

Toiletries and Laundry Gear

As you will see in the next section, I am a fan of taking fewer clothes. The only downside to this approach is you will have to do laundry on a fairly regular basis. How you wash your clothing will depend very much on which country you are in. In Asia, I give them to someone who advertises to wash, dry and fold them for me within 24 hours. It costs about $2 and is a no-brainer! In Australia and New Zealand, I'd use the washing machines and dryers available in most hostels, motels and camping grounds. I'd just save my small coins and buy a small container of washing powder as needed.

In many other countries, I will do my own laundry in the sink and hang it up in the room or bathroom to dry. If you are washing your body, your hair and your clothes, you only need one of the following: soap, shampoo or laundry detergent. I usually use shampoo for all three because it's almost impossible to get soap out of my thick hair, but many men have no problem washing short hair with it.

Two words of warning here:

45

- Don't ever use shampoo in a washing machine – unless you enjoy bubbles all over the floor, that is!

- If you're flying, you really don't want to travel with a highly-perfumed, un-labeled white powder.

As for toiletries, I carry a toothbrush, toothpaste, deodorant and shampoo – and that's it. Most toiletry bags are far too large, so I will often just use a zip-lock plastic bag which also allows for easy-to-see contents. If you do use a special toiletry bag, make sure it's waterproof, both for protection in bathrooms which have showers that soak the entire room and because bottles of liquids have been known to leak or even burst in transit. I carry small containers because none of these items are at all difficult to buy anywhere there are shops.

I don't generally carry a razor as I borrow my partner's, but this brings us to men and shaving. The most compact and lightest solution is provided with disposable razors and shaving oil, which comes in a tiny bottle and lasts months. You may or may not like it, however, so give it a try before you go. A reasonable compromise is old-fashioned shaving soap, which comes in its own container and for which you will also need a brush. Disposable shavers can, of course, be purchased virtually anywhere. Compared to electric shavers, they are lightweight, don't require a plug or a charger and are immune to power cuts and voltage variations.

Specialized Gear

If you are really short-sighted but love to snorkel or dive, you may want to bring a prescription-lens face mask, if you already own one. Even if your eyes are okay and you can get by with the automatic 20% magnification water gives you, if you love to snorkel and have had a trip ruined by poor fitting rented gear, you may well want to consider either bringing your own mask or buying one on arrival. It's not too bulky and can make a huge difference in your enjoyment. Flippers, wet suits, weight belts and other dive gear, on the other hand, are items you are better off renting locally.

If your passion is photography, then by all means bring your camera(s), even if they are valuable and heavy. (Be sure to inquire about coverage for your equipment if you opt for a travel insurance policy.) While some would advise against this, from my perspective, it's your trip and having the best possible photographic memories of it is important. If this is what makes you happy, then you should bring the gear you know and love.

One caveat, though, particularly for camera gear: bring the roughest, oldest, grubbiest looking bag you can find to carry it in. Avoid a bag emblazoned with brand names like "Nikon" as this translates to "steal me" in some parts of the world. Also, you may want to consider swapping out your brand-labeled camera strap for something more discrete and/or to one specially designed to offer protection from a slash-and-run camera thief.

If you enjoy serious hiking, and particularly if the weather may be rough, then you should consider bringing your good gear. For popular hiking destinations, you may well have the option to rent gear on-location, but otherwise you'll want to consider bringing your good boots, weather-proof outerwear and walking poles (but don't try to carry the poles on your flight).

Entertainment

I used to carry physical books to read while traveling. These, along with guidebooks, accounted for a good portion of my bag's weight and consumed nearly half my packing space. I am beyond happy with the advent of eBook readers! I can now take about 3500 books with me on an eReader that's smaller than a single paperback. Since you still can't use readers when the plane is taking off and landing, I might also bring a magazine for that bit. My partner loves crossword puzzles, so he usually has a book of those with him.

I know it's old-fashioned and quaint, but I still keep a physical journal when I travel. I realize phones and netbooks offer other options for this – heck, I could even annotate my guidebook in the eReader – but you'll want to bring a couple of decent pens if you, too, enjoy literally putting pen to paper now and again.

I've also carried cross-stitch and crochet projects in the past. I've seen people carry sketch books and to make drawings and even paintings to document what they are seeing and experiencing as they travel.

If you're serious about learning the local language, you'll need more than a tourist's phrase book. In South America, I carried a good but compact Spanish/English dictionary. If you carry a smartphone, you might want to investigate purchasing a language app for this purpose.

STUFF TO WEAR

The inexperienced traveller's usual approach is to add some of their favourite outfits to a pile on the bed, think about it, and then add some more. After throwing in a few more items "just in case," it's pretty obvious why few people think they can travel with less than two large suitcases.

I know an easier way. List what you are going to be doing on vacation and how often. A beach holiday may include: the beach (duh) (7 days), snorkelling (3 trips), night clubs (5 times) and a fancy restaurant for a special birthday (once). A trip to Europe might include a day hike in the Swiss Alps (one), museum visits (25), general sightseeing (lots) and an invite to the Queen's garden party at Buckingham Palace (or not).

Should you have that invite arranged, ladies will need a hat and gentlemen will require morning dress (and that's not sweatpants and tennis shoes, guys, just so you know). Assuming you are not in that situation, however, casual is the way to go. You are, after all, on vacation. If you're doing just one activity that requires special gear (diving or a wedding, for example), then consider renting the necessary gear at the location rather than carrying it. The basic principal when it comes to clothing is not to carry anything that can't be layered or used in multiple ways.

Now that you know what you will need to dress for on your vacation, you can intelligently consider what you need to pack. Next step: check the weather prediction. If you are planning ahead for a future trip, a simple Google search for "weather in <insert vacation location> in <insert month>" will give you an idea about what to expect. Typically, climates are hot and dry, hot and humid, temperate, cold and wet or cold and dry. We'll address specific climatic variations later, but in general the clothing you'll need can be split into four or five piles:

1. footwear
2. underwear
3. bottoms
4. tops
5. outer and thermal layers (only required for temperate or cold climates)

Some people wonder, "Is it better to buy new stuff to travel with?" There are different ways to approach this question, and you'll need to decide which one works best for you. You might want to buy new, specialized clothing because it will be useful for multiple trips over time. Alternatively, you might want to buy "cheap and cheerful" as you travel, acknowledging those items are likely to wear out quickly and probably won't need to come home with you. Similarly, you might want to take some of your old clothing from home on a one-way trip (e.g., take the pile of underwear that's near the end of its life and throw it out instead of washing it). With the last two options, you'll also end your trip with more souvenir space in your bag.

Footwear

Consider shoes first because they are the hardest things to pack. You need good, comfortable shoes for almost any type of holiday, but shoes are expensive, bulky to pack and sometimes hard to find while traveling. I often travel to warm places, and I never take closed-toe shoes to such destinations anymore. A pair of sandals with good robust soles (Chacos, Tevas or similar), plus a dressier pair of shoes and I'm good to go. This means sometimes I leave home in the winter looking pretty silly at the airport with sandals on (sometimes with socks!), but at least I don't have to carry a bulky pair of shoes that I won't use for the entire trip.

It's worse for men who will sometimes be refused service if they don't have a pair of "proper" shoes in a fancy (or pretentious) restaurant. A pair of black sports shoes may pass muster and are my best recommendation for such instances.

I never carry walking shoes or boots unless I intend to do serious hiking (i.e., a week-long trek through rough terrain). A comfortable pair of broken-in sneakers or sandals will often suffice for day hikes. If you don't wear hiking boots to walk around your own town, why would you wear them on holiday to do the same? The sole of a shoe is far more important than ankle support, so make sure you buy something that's good quality and slip-resistant and will allow you to walk for hours on uneven surfaces.

Also, in most of Asia and Africa, you will need to remove your shoes often – generally every time you enter someone's house, often when you enter shops and always when you enter temples, mosques and even churches. Likewise, after your shoes have deposited loads of beach sand into your hotel room, you'll start to leave your shoes at your own door. Take note that you'll be much happier with shoes which don't require you to sit down to get them off and on.

Intimate Garments

Underwear is relatively easy. Basically you need three to five pairs of underpants/panties/knickers and if you wear a bra, perhaps three of those (they are easier to dry overnight). Sometimes I'll take a pile of nearly worn-out items and just discard them as I need packing space for some souvenirs. I've never bought the specialized "traveler's underwear," preferring a "take what you have and are comfortable with" approach. Do be careful to take colors that don't show under the rest of your clothing, though, and if you're going to a warm clime, do consider cotton or bamboo fabrics that allow your skin to breathe and minimize the risk of a nasty rash.

If you have to take shoes, you will need a couple of pairs of suitable socks, as well. If I don't have shoes, I will sometimes take socks anyway for the plane, for cooler days and/or if the insects are gnawing on me at sunset.

I've never understood the recommendation to take a separate pair of flip flops to wear to the bathroom. Perhaps it's a holdover from the days before Chacos and Tevas existed? If you buy waterproof sandals, they will work equally well in the bathroom, swimming pool, beach or on a wet day.

Bottoms

This includes skirts, shorts or trousers, depending on your gender and the climate. For most people, three different bottoms are plenty. Since bottoms don't get as a dirty as tops, however, you may be able to make do with only two selections. At a minimum, I'll pack a pair of shorts and a sarong that can be worn as a skirt.

For most trips, I pack one pair of casual shorts, one skirt and one pair of trousers. For a man, I'd recommend two pairs of shorts and one pair of trousers (or the other way around on the numbers if the climate is cooler). I do sometimes wear the zip-off style travel pants; they're a reasonable compromise if you're traveling through a few climate zones.

Modern "quick dry" fabrics are good for trousers, particularly if you're going to be out in the rain in cool or temperate climates. But for really hot weather, I prefer shorts and skirts in cotton or cotton-blend fabrics.

The trick is to choose really boring solid colors for the bottom half of your attire. I usually have black trousers (appear more formal than they are), and then dark blue shorts and a patterned skirt. All of my tops go with all of my bottoms. If you are traveling outside popular resort areas in Europe or the Caribbean, I would dress more conservatively. I do wear shorts in such locales, but they are knee length (not cut-offs) and they don't ride low on my hips. I wear skirts, but they are fairly loose and often at least knee length. This is actually as much about comfort as it is about cultural considerations. A pair of loose-cut cotton shorts or a skirt is appreciably cooler than tight denim.

A special note on jeans (or anything made of denim, for that matter): Do not take them! Jeans are too hot to wear in many climates, and they will help get you seriously cold in a really cold climate (unlike wool or modern fabrics which will dry quickly, wet cotton does not retain heat). Jeans are typically too tight to wear another layer underneath, and they can sometimes deny you entry into bars, even ones which have very low standard of dress (a common bar sign in Australia instructs "no jeans, cut-offs, singlets or work boots").

Tops

Most of my tops are shirts, usually with short or long sleeves. Cotton is still the best fabric for a very hot climate – it just breathes so well – and if it's hot, getting it dry won't matter too much. While silk shirts take the least amount of room, they can be fragile (they sometimes really require an iron to look presentable) and the good quality ones are expensive. I compromise on cotton or cotton/poly shirts which are cheap; they roll to a reasonable size and I can buy them almost anywhere.

For a more temperate or cooler climate, then the modern "instant-dry" travel clothes are worth checking out. I find them to be not as comfortable as cotton in very hot climates (despite their claims to the contrary), and they are expensive. They do last reasonably well over lots of washings, though, and are very easy to dry. Your mileage may vary, so try one piece out before you commit to purchasing an entire "instant-dry" travel wardrobe.

Specialty travel clothes do have one huge advantage, particularly for women: pockets. Even if you have a travel day bag or purse with you, pockets are extremely useful and, in women's regular clothing, are often either missing or too small to use. In many developing countries, the currency includes few or no coins, just bills, so I tend to dispense with a wallet and just keep a roll of bills in a pocket. A shirt with button-down pockets is perfect, and this solution is also a lot safer (men take note!) than using a back pocket.

Thick cotton t-shirts are way too hot for most climates but a soft, light T-shirt can be useful to sleep in, particularly if you have a shared bathroom or serious air conditioning – much more useful from my perspective than specialized night clothes. Even in cooler climates, cotton t-shirts are hard to dry and quite inflexible, whereas button-down shirts are more likely to have pockets and can be layered.

GEAR TO WEAR IN THE HEAT

I like hot weather, and like many of you I live in a not very warm part of the country. Packing for warm weather is a delight, the dream of warm things to come!

In warm weather you may sweat through a few more sets of clothes, but at least they're easy to launder, right? Not necessarily; if it's very humid, it can be almost impossible to get things dry without a dryer. In the absence of one, it will take more than 24 hours to get your clothes back from the laundry-lady (Have I mentioned how I love cheap countries where someone else will do my laundry for a dollar or three?) So is this time constraint a disaster? Not from my perspective; just buy another top or spend more time in your swimsuit. Crisis averted.

One thing many people forget to pack for is the ice-cold air conditioning people who live in hot climates often love. I froze once in Dubai in one of their many mega malls. It was 104F (40C) outside, but inside it was more like 59F (15C)! Long-haul buses often suffer from the same problem in Asia and India.

Take a long-sleeved sweatshirt or heavier shirt, and it will double as a pillow if you don't need to wear it. Weather is well worth researching so you can at least approximate rather than assume; for example, did you know it can fall to freezing in the Australian outback in winter (June through August) and Vietnam's winter (November through March) often includes snow in the northern highlands?

Not only is that long-sleeved shirt good for protection against overzealous air-conditioning, but I also often use it as a beach/pool cover-up. No matter how much sunscreen I put on I'll still burn, so I will sometimes swim with a shirt on over my swimsuit.

Another useful trick for layering clothing – and useful for either gender – is to take one sleeveless tank or light T-shirt and then use this under a shirt either for warmth or with the shirt open for effect. Again, chose a color that works well in combination with your other items.

For the girls, a two-piece swimsuit can also work as a second layer and/or underwear. (My wobbly bits are best hidden under a tankini rather than exposed in a bikini!) A one-piece swimsuit is too hard to get in and out of under clothes. Men's swimsuits can double as shorts or underwear, as well, if need be.

I avoid packing sleeveless tops. For both sexes they are deemed highly inappropriate in almost every major religion's buildings: St Peter's in the Vatican, any mosque and/or any Hindu temple will ask you to cover your arms at a minimum, male and female. They also tend to show your money belt (if you're wearing a shoulder holster-style model) and leave your shoulders exposed to uncomfortable rubbing if you're carrying a pack or a day bag over your shoulder. What's more, this rubbing can remove sunscreen you may have applied and leave your shoulders exposed to sunburn. Wear a top with at least short sleeves. In fact, if it's very hot and dry weather, buy a long-sleeved top. The reason most tribes who evolved wandering around deserts cover up is because, in the long run, it's more comfortable and slows down your body's dehydration.

Let's not even think about taking a dress, okay? They are simply too inflexible to have any place in the travel wardrobe, taking up as much space as a top plus a bottom, but will need laundering as often as a top. They're useless for a "travel light" approach. If you want a beach cover up, use either a sarong or one of your long-sleeved shirts/tops.

Bottoms are easy if you are a guy: two pairs of shorts and a pair of trousers. For a girl, the same will do, but I will often carry a skirt instead of the trousers. The skirt is cooler (assuming it's not tight), and it's also often easier to manage in less than hygienic bathrooms (or even just ones with wet floors).

I take cotton or bamboo underwear to warm climes. Trust me on this; you won't regret it. You don't need socks unless you are taking shoes for which they'll be needed (see below).

I usually take one pair of Teva or Chaco sandals (which I wear 95% of the time) and a pair of dressier (i.e., black but still flat) sandals for nicer places. If you're doing a lot of snorkeling and swimming, you may want to bring a pair of reef or dive shoes. They can be very expensive to buy on arrival, particularly at resorts, but cheap to buy at Walmart and then abandon, if necessary. I do lots of walking, but I hate wearing walking shoes or boots in the tropics. My Tevas' good tread will get me most places. (I'm not talking multi-day treks, mind you, more like a short two-hour hike.) Most men will want to take a pair of formal shoes, and then they will probably carry them around the entire trip and never wear them. Take note of this after your first trip, and then feel free to delete them from your next vacation packing list!

I'll talk later about just how useful a sarong is, but if you don't already own one you can buy it on-location.

If you are not used to hot weather, you'll probably need a good sun hat. I don't mean a baseball cap; rather, an actual hat that protects the back of your neck and not just your face. If you don't own one, again they're easily purchased anywhere the weather justifies it. You can get foldaway hats which will survive for years, or you can buy a cheap one which you will likely abandon before your return flight. Either will work, but the latter is better if you have a tendency to lose hats!

I don't carry wet-weather gear for the tropics. Your sweat will make you wetter than the rain! Instead, I will often buy an umbrella and frequently use it like a parasol to keep the sun off. It's a trick I learned in Asia watching the locals (male and female), and it works. As a bonus, it does double-duty if the heavens do open while you're out. I don't buy an expensive travel umbrella before I go, preferring to buy a cheap one when I arrive. It rarely makes it home in one piece, but I get my few dollars' worth out of it.

Swimsuits are non-negotiable. I live to swim, so the swimsuit goes. I do often take a two-piece tankini so I can use it for underwear or even as a dressy top (black works best for this). Men have it easier, regardless of whether they use Speedos (not my favorite, personally, but they do double as underwear) or shorts-style swim trunks.

Another common problem occurs when you're flying from deep mid-winter weather at home to somewhere warm, say New York to the Caribbean during December. Do you take a winter jacket on the entire tropical holiday or risk hypothermia on the way to your home airport? Neither is a particularly pleasing scenario. I prefer to arrange for friends to drop me at the airport and to collect me and then leave my warm coat in their care. You can also sometimes hire a locker for this purpose, and the cost may be justified if it's only a short trip. Or, if your car will remain in long-term parking during the trip, you might also leave your warm clothing – coat, gloves, boots, etc. – inside of it, awaiting your return.

Female Warm-Climate Clothes Packing List

- 1 pair of Chacos or similar sports sandals, preferably waterproof

- 1 pair of flat but dressier shoes (optional for dancing, in my case)

- 5 panties

- 3 bras

- 1 pair of socks

- 1 pair shorts, dark colored

- 1 pair trousers, black

- 1 skirt, multicolored

- 1 lightweight sweatshirt/cardigan/heavier shirt

- 2 short-sleeved shirts

- 1 long-sleeved shirt

- 1 sleeveless tank top

- 1 tankini or bikini

- 1 sarong (doubles as a skirt and beach towel)

- 1 lightweight T-shirt (for sleeping)

Male Warm-Climate Clothes Packing List

- 1 pair of Chacos or similar sandals, preferably waterproof

- 1 pair of formal shoes or dark sneakers (optional)

- 5 underwear

- 2 shorts, dark colors

- 1 pair trousers, dark colored (to get away with as formal)

- 1 lightweight sweatshirt

- 2 short-sleeved shirts

- 1 long-sleeved shirt

- 1 swim shorts (doubles as shorts or underwear, depending on style)

- 1 T-shirt (for swimming or sleeping)

GEAR TO WEAR IN THE COLD

Cold weather is a more expensive to pack lightly for than hot weather, but thanks to the booming travel gear market it's not terribly difficult. In contrast to clothing for warm climates, I'm prepared to pay a bit for the right cold weather gear because it can greatly improve the overall travel experience.

As anyone who has spent any amount of time in the snow will tell you, it's all about layering. You will be much warmer wearing three thin layers than one really heavy layer, so the first thing you leave at home is that heavy, full-length coat you love.

The good news about cold weather packing is that you will be wearing most of the bulky stuff while traveling so it really doesn't need to be packed, per se. This is why I can still carry the same small pack that took me through Thailand in November on my January-in-Europe trip.

My three basic cold-weather layers are:

- thermal underwear
- Merino wool middle layer
- windproof/waterproof outer layer

In between these, I wear lightweight trousers and a lightweight shirt or T-shirt. After adding gloves, hat, socks and some good-soled boots, I was more than warm enough at 14F (-10C) in Prague during December.

The trick is to have thermal underwear tops which don't look like underwear and bottoms that can double as tights. Buy solid colors rather than stripes and get a high-rolled (turtleneck) collar which can provide neck protection like a scarf. Try to color-coordinate your regular tops with your thermal tops if you might be taking the sweater off indoors and in public.

Remember, in a cold climate you won't need to pack your heavy shoes or outer jacket into your luggage; you'll be wearing them! If the climate is variable, you may want a bag that allows you to strap your jacket onto the outside of it when not in use.

In a lot of ways, the laundry is easier in a cold climate, particularly if the indoors are well-heated. Of all those layers, only the inner-most layer's items will need regular laundering.

Probably the best fabric to wear for warmth and comfort is Merino wool, but it's also pretty expensive; silk and polypropylene are less costly alternatives. Merino is highly deceptive. While a thin Merino sweater may not look that warm, combine it with a windproof, waterproof shell jacket and it will not only keep you warmer and dryer than a heavy winter coat or a down jacket, it will pack into a fraction of the space. Although Merino is wool, it's not itchy; this is why it was first adopted by people like river guides who are wet and active all day long. It really will keep you warm when you are sweating, won't smell, is washable (by hand or machine) and will keep its shape. Merino leggings look as good as any, and if you have a longer sweater you can probably get away without the trousers (may be best only for the girls!).

Warm shoes are critical. I don't travel with hiking boots – they're too bulky – but I wear walking shoes or very lightweight boots which have good thick soles which keep the cold out. Dress up is a problem, though, and may require you to carry another pair of formal shoes which tend not to be so warm. You will want to really consider long and hard whether you're going to use these enough to justify packing them. Black always looks more formal, whether you're choosing shoes or trousers.

I choose a jacket with a hood, partly because it helps keep the rain off my glasses, but also if it's really cold it adds another layer of protection. Buy one you can fit a hat under. I also look for something with pockets that my hands will fit in easily, as the covering that pockets afford will often allow me to wear less bulky gloves.

If the hat and gloves aren't needed and don't fit in your bag, put them in pockets of your jacket before you strap that to your luggage. I would count a scarf as purely optional; I don't like them, personally, but my partner always has one in cold weather. You can buy a cheapie if you decide you want one on vacation or take a more expensive pashmina or Merino one with you.

Polar fleece is great – I wear it all the time at home – but I wouldn't take it on holiday. It's too bulky, not warm enough for the bulk involved and hard to dry. You'll be warmer wearing two layers of Merino or similar.

For a temperate climate, I would take one more pair of trousers (replacing the shorts) and another mid-weight layer such as a Merino pullover or sweatshirt (or a jacket, perhaps, depending on the level of formal dressing required). You may want more long-sleeved and fewer short-sleeved shirts, depending on whether you're more likely to be too hot or too cold.

Ever hopeful, I will still carry swim attire when traveling to a cold climate, but in reality it's more likely to be worn as underwear than for swimming. If rain is likely, I'd also pack a lightweight, foldaway rain jacket.

For really cold weather, I'd add hat, gloves (and scarf, maybe), thermal underwear, heavy-duty shoes or light boots, heavier and additional socks and a heavier jacket.

Cold Climate Clothes Packing List

- 1 pair of walking shoes

- 1 pair of Chacos or similar sports sandals, preferably waterproof (optional)

- 1 pair of dressier shoes (optional)
- 5 panties/underwear 3 bras (female only)
- 1 thermal (Merino or polypropylene) leggings
- 1 thermal (Merino or polypropylene) long-sleeved top
- 2 pairs of socks
- 3 trousers (one black for more formal occasions)
- 3 shirts
- 1 mid-layer sweater (Merino or poly-propylene)
- 1 windproof/water-resistant jacket 1 warm hat (optional, depends on how cold)
- 1 pair of gloves (optional, depends on how cold)
- 1 scarf (optional, depends on how cold)
- 1 tankini or bikini or swim shorts (optional)
- 1 sarong (doubles as a skirt and swim towel)
- 1 lightweight T-shirt for sleeping (optional, thermals can work too)

ESTUFF - DO YOU NEED IT?

Cameras and Videos

We've already talked about the dedicated amateur photographer taking their gear, but vacation is usually a prime photo-taking life event for the rest of us, as well. To my eye, smartphones (even iPhones), take pretty substandard photos – it has something to do with the size of the lens, I think – so if you want even moderately good photos, take a camera.

Video cameras used to be hugely popular, but technology has moved on and most still cameras will also take decent video these days should you want to have video memories of your trip.

There are entrie books written on the best cameras for traveling, but I keep it simple. You need a good zoom (the longer the better) and optical is better than digital.

This does rule out the smallest and lightest cameras, but if you're keen on photographing people or even just buildings, you won't regret taking a camera with at least a ten times (10X) optical zoom.

You need a camera with some type of viewfinder (this is also where phones fail as cameras). If it's even slightly sunny, you won't be able to see anything on a screen, however big it is. Rather, go for a smaller screen and make sure there's a viewfinder you can put up to your eye.

Have you ever noticed how camera batteries usually die just as the whales appear in the distance? If you bring a camera, you'll need a spare battery. How you deal with that directly, however, depends on what type of battery your camera takes. If it uses standard AA or AAA batteries, these can be bought literally anywhere in the world. (Depending on the length of our trip, I will either bring a charger for our camera's AA batteries or just buy more batteries if I need them.)

Many cameras have specialized batteries, however, and you'll need to bring your own back up. And, of course, while standard batteries have standard chargers, you may also need a specialized charger for your camera's specialized battery.

Cell Phones

I'm probably showing my age with this, but I do recall when people managed to have a social life without carrying a phone with them all day, every day. If you're traveling within your own country, then taking your phone is probably a no-brainer as you are already paying for the plan. If you are off overseas, however, it's a more complex issue.

Most U.S. phones can't be unlocked; you're tied to using your existing mobile service provider. This can lead to extremely high costs for calls, texts and, in particular, for data transmissions. These data transmission charges occur when you use your phone for email, Facebook, photo sharing or surfing the web, and they can get outrageous in a hurry. (You've been warned!)

For many people in many countries, if you have an unlocked phone you can just arrive in a country, buy a local SIM card, insert it into the phone and you're in business with cheap rates. Your phone number will have changed, though, so you'll need to up date your contacts, of course. This just seems unnecessarily burdensome to me, personally, so I don't carry a phone when I'm on vacation. I tell people to email me if there's a problem.

Laptops, Netbooks, iPads, etc.

I travel with a 10″ screen netbook – it cost less than $300 – and if it was lost or stolen or broken on my next trip, my insurance would cover it. Because I'm diligent about backing up the netbook, the data on its hard drive would be accessible, as well, either online (backed up "in the cloud") or on a separate hard drive (about the same size and weight as a very slim paperback). The keyboard is (just) large enough for me to touch type on, and I don't carry any other extras except for a charger and a good padded cover. I need the netbook because I run my business from the road when I travel. It's not nearly as powerful as my main laptop, but it weighs and cost much less, too. The main point is: if it was lost, it wouldn't be a huge issue for me, because I wouldn't lose the data on it.

Unless you work on vacation, I don't believe you need any variant of a laptop. If you want to check emails occasionally, use an Internet cafe. They're everywhere. If this option doesn't appear to be available in your specific destination, then your chances of being able to connect to the Internet with your own laptop there are slim to none anyway. Many will argue, especially if they're doing a longer trip, they need to "stay connected." Why? Let people know you will offline for a while, and then actually concentrate on being in the place where you're spending good money to be. I believe it's called "living in the now," but I just call it living sensibly.

eReaders: Kindle, Nook, Kobe, etc.

In terms of travel, eBooks are an absolute no-brainer. While I'd suggest you buy a protective pouch or cover for travel, eReaders are robust and weigh less than any paperback or other electronic device. A Kindle will run for nearly a month on one charge. They rock. You might also be reading this on your smartphone, iPad or on a laptop/netbook; if you've decided to take one of those other devices on your vacation, you really don't need to bring a dedicated eReader. Remember: travel light.

Plugs and Power

If you take electronics, they'll need charging. If you are using them abroad, it won't be as simple as plugging them into the wall. There are two issues; one is simple, and the other is not.

First, we must consider voltage. A lot of the world uses 220V, while the U.S. and much of the rest of the Americas use 110V. Modern electronics – particularly phones, laptops and items specifically designed for travel (e.g., travel hair dryers) – are often labeled "dual voltage" and in (very) fine print you will see 110V/220V or 220V/110V or even 220-240V/110V, all of which are good news for the traveler. Check this before you leave home, as it is NOT okay if you are going to a 220V country with a strictly 110V appliance (or vice versa). Just so we're clear, it will be "NOT okay" in a "shower of sparks and death to the appliance" sort of way, so be VERY sure about this aspect of traveling with your expensive electronics.

You can get voltage adapters, of course, but they're heavy, expensive and may not work well. Also, any appliance that creates a lot of heat (like a heater or a dryer) will likely blow a voltage adapter.

The other issue is a physical one. Plugs come in numerous shapes and sizes – 3 pin, 2 pin, round pins, fat pins, thin pins – and your plug may not physically fit in the sockets available at your destination. Even within a country, you may see a variety of different plug receptacles. I've even seen different types of outlets within the same room! Although it's nice to get a combination plug adapter which will cover the world, if you can't find one or are only going to visit one country it may be easier to just buy an adaptor upon arrival.

Cables and plugs can add a surprising amount of bulk and weight to your travel load, so try and streamline and, if possible, coordinate and share these items with a traveling partner. For example, if both your Kindle and your partner's smartphone can charge off a USB cable and you're carrying a laptop, you don't need to bring those individual devices' plug-in chargers; just bring the USB cable and use the laptop.

By now you should have the basis for determining a reasonable list of requirements for any trip. You know to focus on the important things; that your first priority is documents, money and access to the same. Security and health come next, while clothing is lower on the list since it can be easily replaced anywhere in the world. "If in doubt, leave it out" is a key concept from our clothing discussion.

Finally, we looked at electronics, and I want to encourage you to apply the same key concept to those items. Remember: take what you need, but nothing more. I also hope you're starting to get the idea of how to answer your own packing questions. After a brief recap, let's look at some specific tips and tricks I've developed over my 30 years of traveling.

KEY POINTS: THE WHAT OF PACKING

* Documents, money/cards and prescription medicines are the essentials on your packing list. For the most part, the rest is just fluff. Look after and backup
* the essentials as much as you can.
* Work out what you will be doing while away and then plan clothing for those adventures. Don't take stuff "just in case." Ever.
* You can travel indefinitely with three outfits – really, you can, I promise!
* You really don't need any electronics, although most will take a camera. Again, consider carefully if you really need to "stay connected" on vacation.
* If some of the items mentioned in this chapter are unfamiliar to you then check out http://NonBoringTravelGuides.com/resources

PART 3: PACKING LISTS, TIPS AND TRICKS

So far, I've given you a basic framework for what you will need and, more importantly, what you don't need to pack. In this chapter, we'll discuss some tips and tricks that should allow you to finalize your packing list for an upcoming trip and to refine that list for future travels. Much to the chagrin of the travel accessory industry, I'm sure, this chapter is also where you're going to save yourself a lot of money. First, let's talk about whether you need a list at all, and then we'll cover some useful stuff I never travel without and a lot of useless stuff I don't think you'll ever need.

To List or Not to List

So do you need a vacation packing list? Amusing as it may be given the title of this book, I don't actually use a packing list. As I generally travel to warm places in the middle of winter, I'm typically traveling with stuff I don't wear from day to day. So, about a week before we're due to leave, I start to pack. I work out what clothes I want and make sure they're in reasonable condition. I double check to ensure I have the really important stuff sorted out (passport not expired, credit cards not expiring while away, itinerary and reservation information printed, etc.), backup my netbook drive, prepare the camera and assemble all the cables and plugs necessary to make them work at my destination.

While I don't use a list, I have been doing this for quite a while and with regular frequency. For the less experienced, I do suggest you start with a list. Compile one and work from it as you pack for your trip. When you return, go back over the list and cross off anything you didn't use, add anything you bought and brought home and make notes as to what worked and what didn't. (Try to do this on the flight home before you get busy being back and forget the useful things you learned along the way.) Then, leave the list in your travel bag, awaiting your next vacation.

Until now, we've talked about packing suggestions and requirements as if you were traveling solo and with the same gear accompanying you for the whole trip. There are some variations which might work better for certain circumstances, however, so let's touch on those a bit.

Packing with a Friend

If you are traveling with a friend, partner or spouse, there's quite a lot of stuff you don't need two sets of –

electronics, laundry stuff, some toiletries, first aid kit, books, etc. – since you can share. If you are a family traveling, you may even be able to share more, say sharing one charger between four people.

Bag Drop

This is handy if your trip is split between two distinct climates; for example, you've planned a warm tropical stopover en route to a more temperate destination. For an efficient approach, try to arrange an overnight in the same city at the start and end of one part of your trip. Carry a third bag (or buy a cheap one there) and arrange to leave this bag (into which you've placed the clothing you don't need for the next leg) with your overnight lodging location. Every hotel I've ever been to will hold a small bag for a guest who has a future reservation, but it's probably even worth a few dollars not to have to tote unnecessary items to your next stop.

For what it's worth, I wouldn't leave expensive items in that bag, but it's highly unlikely anyone is going to steal your cold weather clothing in a hot climate (or vice versa). In general, leaving a bag at an airport is not a good idea – many airports no longer allow it anyway – and any that do allow it charge a small fortune. Using a train station locker or left-luggage storage facility may work in some parts of the world, but using your hotel is the easiest of all.

Parcel Home

A variant of the bag drop method is mailing home what you no longer need. This is rarely economically sensible for cheap clothes, but it may be worth it if the items in question are expensive winter gear. For cheap stuff, I just abandon them in the hotel or give them away on the street in very poor countries.

Buy a Bag

The opposite, of course, is starting light and then going on a shopping spree later in the trip. Many places which make a lot of money by selling stuff to tourists will also sell you a bag to transport it all home. (Some even offer to pack and mail it on your behalf, but this requires a bit more trust than I have.) After one particularly fruitful tailor-made, custom clothing expedition in Vietnam, we had the shop package it all into a couple of cheap bags. They did such a good job that my only concern was customs at some border might want to see inside after which I'd have to attempt to repack it. Fortunately, this didn't happen. I also remember how telling a carpet salesman in Turkey his rug was too big to pack led to an amazing packing demonstration – and I still have the rug to remind me of it!

SECURITY IS (MOSTLY) IN YOUR MIND

Security is a lot more about attitude than gear. If you walk around expecting to be mugged, your fears may well be realized; you will look fearful and cautious and appear an attractive target. "Fake it until you make it" really does apply to looking confident on the street! One time when I was pretty sure I was being shadowed down a street in Brazil, I did a U-turn and walked back toward the tracker, who took to his heels and ran away! Don't walk around oblivious to your surroundings, and PLEASE don't walk in busy places with earphones plugging your ears. This is just asking for trouble. While that advice won't make packing easier, it might keep you from becoming a traffic statistic!

Don't take the "faking it" concept too far, though, thinking you can leave your common sense at home. Don't walk down dark alleys at 3am by yourself, particularly if you're drunk. You wouldn't do that at home, would you? Understand that when you travel, particularly to poorer countries, you go from being an ordinary, middle-class citizen who speaks the language to a rich tourist who's permanently lost and can't communicate well. This makes you vulnerable and you need to manage that risk, but not in the way most people think.

While your chance of being held-up and robbed is low, what's far more likely to occur is an opportunistic theft. For example, someone grabs a bag you leave unattended on the curb while it's waiting to be loaded on a bus or someone takes your wallet from your back pocket without you noticing. Luckily, there are things you can do to avoid opportunistic theft.

Carrying Your Cash and Passport

First and foremost, never, ever carry all your valuables in one place. I don't mean your camera and iPhone, by the way; while they're expensive, they're also easily replaced. The really valuable stuff is your cash, cards and passport. My passport and the majority of my cash and cards travel next to my skin, where I can feel them and know they're there.

Money belts are popular, but in reality no one wears them. They're uncomfortable and hot to wear. If you aren't wearing them, then you might as well just use a wallet. Neck pouches are equally uncomfortable (more so for some women) and even more obvious. Again, they usually end up just being thrown into your day bag. Two options that do work:

- A shoulder, holster-style money carrier which hangs under your arm. It's hard to see (assuming you aren't wearing tight clothing) and it's not so close to your body that it will rub and make you hot.
- You can get pockets that clip onto the inside of your trousers' waistband or onto an arm or leg. I don't use them because they aren't big enough for my rigid passport, but they do work for money and cards.

I carry most of my money in my shoulder holster, but not all of it. If you're traveling alone, you need to make sure you have a backup plan in case of emergency – a few hundred dollars cash and maybe a second card not associated with your first card's account (because that first account will be frozen if you have to report its card as missing).

I put this backup reserve somewhere deep in my bag – and not my day bag, my main bag. It goes inside a book or in with the socks, somewhere that's not obvious. A few $50 bills under a shoe innersole works, too (swap them from time to time). At night, I sleep with my money holster under my pillow.

If you're traveling with a partner, don't have one person carry all the money and passports. Couples make this mistake all the time. You should both carry your own passport, some of the money and separate cards to split the risk.

I often carry a wallet. While you don't necessarily need to, you do need to be able to easily access limited amounts of cash. There's no point wearing a discrete money belt with $1000 in it if you then must pull it out in the middle of a market to pay for a 50c drink! Carry a day-or-two's worth of cash in a pocket or a wallet. I've had my wallet stolen by pickpockets several times, but since I limit what I carry in it I've never lost more than a little money.

Swimming is a problem since passports don't swim well. There are, however, waterproof money belts (like mini-dry bags) available, and I've used those. Unless the hotel room is very seriously scary, I lock my passport and other valuables in the bottom of my main pack when I go swimming and leave that at the hotel.

Speaking of hotel security, maybe I'm really psychic, but I doubt it. I get a feeling about whether a hotel is safe or not quite quickly. If it's obviously family-run and people make eye contact and smile, that's a good start. It doesn't guarantee someone won't break into your room, but it makes it far less likely because basically there will be people around during the day.

Sadly, if you're on the hostel circuit and using dorms, the biggest risk of theft is from fellow travelers. Frankly, I'd be very discrete with anything that's trendy. Keep any new Mac, iPhone, tablets and other cool tech stuff out of sight. Grubby bags might also help deter this group of thieves.

Don't go chaining your bag in your room, screaming "money here!" and making it hard for the cleaners to do their job, either.

You're much better off hiding valuables in the bottom of a discretely locked main bag, as your main bag is more unlikely to be stolen in its entirety. It's simply too hard for the thief to leave with it unnoticed.

A SHORT LIST OF USEFUL TRAVEL GEAR

As promised, this will be a short list: A **travel alarm clock,** small with a built-in light, with an easy-to-set alarm can be useful. Even if you can normally wake up at a regular time at home, you may need an alarm clock on the road. I nearly missed checking out of a hotel on time once. I was sound asleep, thanks to jet lag, at 10am and hadn't thought to use the alarm! Yes, I know your phone has an alarm, but do you really want your phone on, particularly if you're in an odd time zone? If you regularly use your watch's alarm, that will do; just don't wait until vacation to learn how to set the alarm and change the time. The simple lightweight alarm I carry is very easy to use.

A small **LED flashlight** is nice to have, and LED flashlights last a lot longer on a couple of batteries than the old-style bulbs. I currently use an LED headlight-style flashlight which I like because it's better for reading in bed. Even quite good hotels overseas often have really poor bedside lighting, and I love to read so this is an essential for me. It can also come in handy in destinations where poor street lighting or frequent power cuts are the norm. It weighs next to nothing, but you're better off with one that's hard to turn on (so it won't turn itself on in your bag) and that takes regular AA or AAA batteries (available anywhere there are shops).

A **universal sink stopper** is basically just a flat piece of rubber so it will fit any sink. If you're wondering why this is on the list, just imagine trying to wash clothes in a sink without a stopper. It's useful for shaving, too. While virtually indestructible, I have lost a few over the years by unintentionally leaving them behind.

A **travel clothesline** is also a useful item for laundry purposes. This is basically two pieces of twisted elastic (which means you don't need pegs) that will stretch to fit the weirdest situations. Again, almost indestructible, one should last for decades.

A **sarong**. Douglas Adams stated in his *Hitchhiker's Guide to the Universe* that you should never leave home without a towel, and I've adapted this slightly for my purely earth-bound explorations. I never leave home without a sarong. It's simply the world's most multi-purpose item of clothing/gear. The list of things I've used a sarong for include:

- skirt (acceptable for men in many countries to)
- dress
- towel (beach or otherwise)

- beach cover up
- top sheet on a bed
- shawl (sun-protection or warmth)
- head covering (for mosques and churchs)
- shoulder covering for temples (Buddhist and Hindu)
- carry bag for dirty laundry
- picnic cloth
- nightdress
- curtain (in conjunction with traveler's clothesline above)

Getting the right sarong is important. You can get some that are shaped with ties, but I find the standard rectangle works best. Pure cotton, oddly, doesn't work that well as it rips too easily and won't tie tightly enough. Poly/cotton mixes are better in my experience, but the cheapest rayon sarongs really are one-trip wonders and rip easily when wet.

A **water-resistant pack cove**r is sometimes built in to a pack's design, but you can buy them separately, as well. These are great, of course, if you get caught in the rain when out walking, but often in Asia and Africa packs will go on the top of mini-vans and buses (even a small bag) and frequently without the benefit of a tarpaulin. The pack covers will help keep your bags clean, too.

A LONGER LIST OF USELESS TRAVEL GEAR

Topping the list of stuff you don't need: a **mosquito net**. I can't believe people are still voluntarily walking around with mosquito nets. You didn't need them 30 years ago when I first backpacked in Asia, and that was before hotel standards improved. While I've certainly spent many nights under mosquito nets and consider them a necessity at several destinations I love, all but the most basic hotel/guest house will provide them if you need them.

A **sleeping bag** is a close second. I would probably still take a lightweight one for trekking in Nepal, but if you're traveling in Europe or Asia, definitely not. Unless you're actually camping (in which case you need quite a lot more than a sleeping bag), you don't need a sleeping bag. If it's warm, a sarong is a good substitute – and a lot lighter to carry. Further, sleeping bags are banned in most decent hostels in the UK, Singapore and Australia (to prevent bed bug infestations), but you may need a sheet sleeping bag (silk ones are very compact) for those destinations.

Current fashion dictates that you should carry **duct tape**. I've seen this recommended on numerous travel forums, but I'm yet to figure out what you are actually supposed to use it for. If you do find a use for it, buy it on the spot and please enlighten me. I truly don't get it.

Towels Unless you are traveling ultra-cheap (i.e., a dormitory-style accommodation), most hotels these days will provide a towel. Even when we are staying at a "flash-packer" level accommodation – although we always stay in a private room rather than dorms – we are almost always provided towels. On occasion, however, we've had to make do with a sarong or pay a towel fee. If you expect to need a towel regularly, then I'd buy a travel towel – not a huge one, mind you, as small one will do just fine. While they aren't quite the same as wrapping yourself in a warm fluffy towel, they do the job.

Water bottles. Following the same logic which persuades people who live in countries with perfectly drinkable tap water to pay lots of money on bottled water, why not take an empty water bottle with you? Much of the world has water you shouldn't drink from the tap, and that's why in those countries you will find bottles full of drinking water for sale on every street corner. Buy a bottle, buy several, each one will come with a plastic bottle. Reuse the bottle if you find a clean source, but you still don't need to bring a bottle from home! Expert trick: some bottles are better than others, as are some caps. Pay attention and find the local brand which is least likely to spray water throughout your bag.

Pacsafes and **pack alarms**. Pacsafes have been around for a while. They are constructed of a metal "slash proof" mesh that's provided as an external covering or, alternatively, already woven into a bag's fabric. While the theory is fine, the problem is that in all my years of traveling I've only met two people who had a bag slashed. One had a money belt slashed on a crowded Bolivian bus, and the other was a girl whose bag was damaged, but from which nothing was stolen, when slashed on a crowded street in Italy. Just to be clear: I've met many people who have had a bag snatched because they recklessly turned their back, left it locked in a car or stupidly put it on the back of a chair while sitting in a street cafe in La Paz, Bolivia (that last one was me, by the way). Slashing is just not a very efficient or easy way to steal anything of value, so Pacsafes market directly to our fear of the world and address a problem that really doesn't exist to any great extent. They are also expensive, heavy and, from my perspective, scream "steal me – I'm valuable and have expensive stuff inside!" Personally, I consider Pacsafes a thief magnet rather than a deterrent.

Padlocks with keys. Now padlocks are great and you should make sure you buy bags that have zippers that can be locked together, but the keys are a nightmare. Instead, get a combination lock, and be sure to get a TSA-approved one if you'll be flying through U.S.

airports. Set all your combinations alike – to something very memorable and personal. (I use the first digits of my birth date.) Don't buy the new ones with cards. Each lock has its own card, and how are you supposed to know which one goes with which lock? It's beyond me!

Here are some more ways I've seen people waste money: Small containers for carry-on liquids. I'm not saying you mustn't have small containers to be allowed to carry on liquids to planes. You do need these, of course, but you don't need to buy empty containers which make it difficult to get your liquid of choice into them and then require you to remember which is your shampoo and which is your hand sanitizer! Instead, I collect hotel-sized toiletries when I travel and/or will buy small containers of a required product, as needed.

Pack cubes. These are cool if someone gives them to you, but I wouldn't actually spend money on what a plastic bag has been doing forever.

Travel laundry bags. Again, a plastic bag will work fine, and it doesn't even matter whether or not it comes back from the laundry. Bonus! Specialized Travel Soap and Laundry Soap. This stuff tends to be over-priced for what is essentially shampoo or unscented soap. It no doubt works, but so does real soap or shampoo for maybe 10% of the price.

What, No Specialized Packing Lists?

You may have noticed how other packing lists and books on the subject spend many, many pages detailing Honeymoon packing tips, Cruise packing tips, packing for kids, long-term packing tips, etc., etc. Me? I'm only going to spend a fraction of that telling you this is all marketing nonsense. It's all about creating "an ultra-niche" and convincing people that, for example, you as a one-legged person recently married to a gay partner have different packing requirements than the next person. You don't. I promise.

Honeymoon packing. Well, if you have been living together for a while, then traveling together for your honeymoon will be pretty much the same as your previous travels together. In fact, it will be exactly the same. If you haven't traveled together before, then consider what items you can share and remember to have your paperwork in order (e.g., your passport name must match your airline booking). Traveling for a long time.

Many people think they need to take different (or, to be blunt, more) stuff with them for a six-month, round-the-world backpacking trip than for a ten-day vacation. They don't need to take more. The same four tops and three bottoms can get you all the way around the world. Mind you, it's very unlikely you will return with the SAME tops and bottoms that you left home with if you go all the way around the world, but you don't actually need any more dirty laundry to carry.

Traveling with a family is like traveling as a couple, but more so. You get to share more stuff between you. Why on earth would someone want to take even more with you? Maybe substitute a Nintendo for a book for the kids, but otherwise please proceed as previously detailed.

So, we now know what we're going to take. We've selected some clothes – not too many – and we have a minimum of toiletries along with our essential prescription medications. We have some idea about which cards to bring and which documents are important.

Let's recap briefly and then look at the finer details of what we're going to take it all in. Let's find some luggage and discuss how best to pack it.

KEY POINTS: TIPS AND TRICKS

- Coordinate your packing list with your travel companion(s) so you don't double up.
- Consider sending some bags home or buying more along the way rather than starting with spare capacity.
- Safety is more about your attitude and minding some sensible precautions than about gear. If you are not going to wear your money belt 24/7, then don't bother having one.
- Consider taking: a travel alarm, flashlight, universal sink stopper, travel clothesline, sarong.
- Don't consider taking: a mosquito net, sleeping bag, large towel, water bottle, Pacsafe.

PART 4: LUGGAGE AND HOW TO PACK IT

Most packing books start with a long discussion about luggage, but that's simply the wrong way to approach the topic. Now that we've worked out how to develop a sensible packing list so you can gauge exactly what you want to take, we can finally have a sensible discussion about what to take it in. In this security conscious world, we also need to talk about whether you should actually carry on your carry-on sized luggage.

THE DEBATE: RIGID CASE OR BACKPACK?

The debate about luggage is never ending. Some swear by hard-sided cases, others by soft bags, some want rollers while others prefer shoulder straps. What's best? Well, as usual, it depends on what you are carrying and, in particular, the weight of it. Let's first consider what your main piece of luggage should be. If you've developed a light list as I've suggested throughout this book, you'll probably be able to fit all your items into a carry-on sized bag. Whether or not you DO actually choose to carry it on is another discussion, and we will cover that later.

Rigid or Hard-Shell Suitcases

These are basically designed to protect the contents. If you have fragile and/or easily crushed items (shoes or hats, for example), then a rigid case may work best. The downside is, of course, that it's rigid, and whether it's 50% full or 110% full it takes up the same amount of space. Some have a minor expansion sleeve, but they are pretty much the same size either way. The advantage of these cases is that, apart from the apparently better protection (I say apparently because a cheap case will break much sooner than a cheapish soft-sided bag), they are easy to pack and easy to find stuff in.

The disadvantage, particularly of the larger cases, is that it's pretty hard to find the right piece of furniture, other than the bed, upon which to place it to open it up and retrieve items. Suitcases are really designed for travelers who plan to unpack them when they arrive at their destination and then repack them upon departure. This could work on a cruise and/or if you regularly stay at superior hotels and regularly stay put on your travels.

If you don't want to completely unpack your belongings when you reach your accommodation, however – perhaps you're moving on every few days – then this becomes a major nuisance rather quickly.

The days of suitcases without wheels are long gone. If it's a rigid-sided bag, it will have wheels in addition to carry handles. Wheels work well indoors on most surfaces and are generally great for traversing long airport corridors' very smooth surfaces. Wheels are a massive fail, though, as soon as you get onto uneven ground. Sand is the worst, but cobblestones are challenging, too. Apparently larger wheels are more stable, and they are very awkard to get up the stairs.

Pulling a bag behind you that has any serious weight to it is also really bad for your back and shoulder. People think they can't carry a pack because of a bad back, but a properly fitting pack will put almost no strain on your back and is a lot better for those with back issues than a pull-along or push-along case.

Any form of rigid case is heavier than the equivalently sized soft-sided bag, and a wheeled bag is always heavier than a non-wheeled equivalent.

Soft Luggage

Many people think a backpack is something you take wilderness hiking, and that's certainly where their popularity developed. But today's modern travel packs are a much improved version of their hiking ancestors. A good travel pack will combine a properly fitted and balanced harness with a pack which is easy to open up and get into. The traditional hiking pack offers only an opening at the top (a design championed to keep the weather out when used in the wilderness), and it's a nuisance for day-to-day packing and unpacking.

A modern travel pack, on the other hand, is more rectangular in shape and will often offer full-length zippers and/or multiple compartments. I also like to have enough outside straps so I can carry a jacket, a wet towel or a pair of wet shoes on the outside rather than inside the pack. (Obviously, when you're flying everything needs to be inside the pack.)

A good backpack will fit you well and provide a good, padded waist belt. This is where all the weight should sit – on your hips rather than your shoulders – and for this reason, your ideal pack length is determined by your shoulder-to-hip measurement. For general travel, you don't want a pack that extends over your shoulder height as this will make you top-heavy. (Packs like that are usually specialized designed for climbing.)

Try a few packs on – with weight in them – in a shop to find a brand and style that suits you. Typically, one brand will work better for you than others. A travelpack will also have double zips so that they can be secured with a small lock.

Note that many packs are 3050 cu in (50L) or up, but this is too much for most people to carry comfortably and far more space than you need for your light travel list. I prefer an 1800-2440 cu in (30-40L) pack. These are often sold as day packs, and finding one with a sturdy enough waist belt can sometimes be tricky as day packs often have a very light belt (which will cut into you if you have some weight in the bag) or no belt at all (which will ruin your shoulders and neck even if you are only carrying an 18lb (8kg) load).

A well-fitting backpack, properly packed (discussed in the next section), should be comfortable for hours, although it's unlikely you'll actually carry it for that long. Although they are currently fashionable, I don't recommend getting a backpack with wheels.

Wheels add an enormous amount of weight and you need a rigid handle, as well, to drag it which adds even more. They're also not terribly comfortable to carry, and the wheels will get your back dirty unless the pack is very carefully designed.

Day Bags

So, apart from your main piece of luggage, what else should you carry? Even though I carry one main bag, I almost always have a second small day bag, as well. Even if you carry your main bag on your flight, it's likely you'll want a second, smaller bag for easy access to some items en route and to use as a day bag during your trip. I have a collapsible one which tucks into its own pocket, weighs nothing and is yet to rip after over five years of tough traveling. You may not get as lucky, but you need something that will carry a water bottle, guidebook and whatever else you need for a day's sightseeing. Mine also doubles as a camera bag on the go.

Try to avoid carrying specialized camera bags and laptop bags, as they are a thief targets. The best way to avoid having stuff stolen is to make it appear as if you have nothing worth stealing. Both my camera and my netbook are in padded, well-fitting, closed-cell foam cases, but they are also both inside other bags, generally in a small shoulder bag I take everywhere. While the bag could definitely use a good wash, it will remain dirty – deliberately.

HOW TO PACK

Having reduced the amount of what you must carry to a reasonable level and found a suitable bag to carry it in, how do you pack? It depends somewhat on the type of bag you have, and it's more critical for a backpack than a roll-along that the weight distribution is correct. For a backpack you need the heaviest items against your back and higher rather than lower in the pack. You will likely need to experiment for yourself with this a bit, but basically you don't want the bag to change your natural center of balance too much. If you feel your bag pushing you forward or dragging you back, it's not packed right.

To Pack a Pack for Your Back

First pack anything light and bulky at the bottom: sleeping bag, a down jacket or similar items are perfect, but if you're not carrying any of those, clothing goes in first. I've heard good things about compression systems, but basically I use a roll method which works fine. I take, for example, trousers and fold them until I have the width I want (the width of the pack) and then I roll them tightly. I do this with all my larger clothing items. I keep my underwear all together in a bag. If you really love pack cubes then use them for organization, but I find reasonable quality plastic bags work fine, too.

Next, I add shoes: light sandals can go right at the bottom of the pack, but heavier shoes may need to go on top of the clothes. I have broken fragile items when I've carelessly dropped a pack down on a hard surface, so I try to pad the bottom of the bag well and make sure it's packed tightly enough so that small fragile items (like chargers) can't fall through to the bottom. In general, I try to pack "like with like." If you don't want your shoes squashed, stuff them with socks or other small soft items to support them internally.

I will have a waterproof (or at least water-resistant) bag or folder for my travel paperwork which will usually slide conveniently down the back of a pack. Be aware, however, that it's possible to sweat through a pack and make it slightly damp inside, so do put important papers inside something plastic.

If I am carrying fragile electronics like my netbook, those goes in next, riding against the back but padded by the papers. The netbook itself is in a well-fitting, drop-resistant sleeve. A small plastic bag holds my various electronic accoutrements – items like plug adapters, a USB cable (for charging my eReader or phone from the netbook), bank security token, etc. – all together and is positioned in the middle of the pack to pad it well. You could use a padded postal envelope to protect small items like a spare disk drive.

From there on, the rest of my clothing is used to pad the fragile stuff in the middle and to balance weight. It's a lot easier now that I carry an eReader rather than four or five paperbacks. I generally put my toiletries bag near the top, although not the very top (even when I carry my pack on the plane, items on top can get crushed). Making the top layer your dirty laundry, paperbacks or the like is useful for dealing with this issue, and it also could deter an opportunistic thief. It's often more efficient to pack smaller items rather than larger. Rather than having a large toiletry bag which includes my first aid kit and laundry items, I split those items between three separate bags.

Packing a Roll-Along Case

This is almost the opposite of packing a bag for your back. With this design, you want the weight at the bottom of the bag to avoid speed wobbles, and you also want to make sure that the weight is balanced so that the bag doesn't pull or curve to one side.

CARRY IT ON? MAYBE, MAYBE NOT

Carry-on luggage can be a hugely confusing issue, particularly if you travel internationally. Every airline seems to have different rules regarding the number of allowed carry-ons, their allowed weight and whether or not a handbag counts as part of your total allowance.

The one thing most airlines seem to agree on is size: the overall dimensions of your carry-on bag should be less than 45in (114cm) or 46in (118cm) with limits on individual dimensions (which means you can't take a very long and skinny bag). At present, the weight limit ranges from 15lbs (7kg) to 22lbs (10kg), but personal observation would seem to indicate you have to be unlucky or obviously struggling with the bag to have your carry-on weighed.

In addition, most airlines allow you to carry one other "personal item" – a purse, small laptop bag or briefcase

– but this is not the case for some budget airlines in Europe. Please note that these carry-on details will apply only to full-size commercial jetliners. If you're traveling on a small, regional airline's plane, your carry-on options will likely be quite limited. Even the security screening requirements vary on different continents.

Current American TSA rules have relaxed a bit, allowing you to travel with small (less than 4" blades) scissors. At present, however, you can't have any scissors in carry-ons when traveling to or from Australia and New Zealand. In an effort to protect the local agricultural industry, you can't bring any food into these countries, either, unless it's sealed and declared. This is not just a carry-on rule, by the way, and forgetting you have a piece of fruit in your bag can result in a large local fine in many countries.

To be on the safe side and considering the current regulations, I'd suggest you do the following. First, review and confirm your airline's carry-on rules. If you're using multiple carriers for a trip, check each one and then be prepared to abide by the most restrictive requirements regarding weight and prohibited items. If you're really pushing the weight limit, you may be able to get away with carrying heavy items (like books) in your coat pockets. If you decide to strictly carry on, double-check the size of any "liquids" you must carry (this includes gels and creams) to ensure they are smaller than 3oz (100ml). If you want to take shampoo etc., just take sample or hotel-sized toiletries (I keep a collection of these for the purpose) to cover the start of your trip and then buy a bigger bottle at your destination. You can simply abandon or give away the unused portion of these purchases before you leave.

Either way, you will need to separate your liquids, if any, and present them to security in a clear, re-sealable bag that's no larger than 1 quart (1 liter) in size. Pack this at the top of your bag or in an external pocket so you can retrieve it easily when you need to present it for the airport security screening. Zip-lock bags, by the way, are perfect for many travel purposes, and I always carry a few spares in varying sizes stashed somewhere in my bag. If you aren't carrying your main luggage on (you are checking it, instead) and particularly if you have connecting flights, beware that luggage does go missing. Usually, it's just a delay rather than a total disappearance, but that can still be quite inconvenient.

This is also why you should always carry all important documents and all essential medicines with you on all flights. I usually have some Tylenol with me, as well, and it can be nice to take a change of underwear as some overseas airports will allow you to shower for a small fee. Changi, Singapore even has a swimming pool, so be sure to pack your swimsuit in your carry-on if you're headed there!

Most airlines will make you turn off your phone, eReader, iPod, iPad and/or laptop for take-off and landing, so you may want to take some dead-tree reading matter. I usually collect some magazines or newspapers I want to catch up with and just dispose of them when finished. Whether it's best to check your carry-on sized luggage can really only be decided on a case-by-case (sorry) basis. I often do, just so I don't have to carry it around the airport, but if I have a tight connection I'll generally carry on so as not to have to worry about a luggage delay.

On the other hand, you'll almost certainly save fees if you carry on with most airlines these days. I have both hard cases and soft bags that I use regularly, but they are for very different styles of travel. A trip that involves lots of flying and/or requires me to utilize public transport means I travel with the lightest possible bag. If you have your own vehicle, though, or will be renting one at your destination, then you can afford to take a bit more with you. After a brief recap of the main points for this final chapter, read on for further resources.

KEY POINTS LUGGAGE PACKING

- Choose your luggage to fit your packing list, not the other way around.
- Pulling a wheeled bag is much harder on your back than carrying a lightweight, well-fitting backpack.
- Roll your clothes to make them compact and use clothing to pad fragile items.
- Even if your total luggage is small enough to carry on (which it should be), be sure to consider the carry-on rules for all the airlines your trip requires before you decide whether to carry or check your luggage.

ABOUT THE AUTHOR

Elisabeth has been traveling since she was seven. Her mother was ill and in the days before dads could look after their kids, she was packed off to a holiday in Ireland with relatives. Elisabeth doesn't remember the trip, but she does remember the excitement of catching her first flight, unaccompanied! These days Elisabeth finds airports and long-haul flights as exciting as a wet Sunday, but she still loves showing up at the airport for the start of a new travel adventure.

Elisabeth has traveled to every continent except Antarctica and that's on the list. She has traveled solo, with friends and with her partner. She's stayed in hostels the fleas weren't impressed with and luxury resorts. She has seen the travel industry evolve from the days before Internet when the only information on a remote destination was a guide book years out of date, to today's twitter-driven instant feedback, well-connected online experience. She's not convinced that this is all good.

These days Elisabeth writes in the back bedroom, in New Zealand's capital city Wellington, with easy access to the airport and the world. Elisabeth is a writer, developer and promoter of websites about various topics, but travel is still her passion.

The Non-Boring Travel Guides series is her attempt to share her love and knowledge of travel with the world

A REQUEST FROM THE AUTHOR

I hope you have enjoyed *The Non-Boring Vacation Packing Guide*. If you've got a minute I'd really appreciate it if you left an honest review of it at Amazon. Book reviews help other readers decide on the books they love, and it would mean a lot to me. Thank you, Elisabeth

SIGN UP FOR A FREE FREE TRAVEL NEWSLETTER

Want to keep up to date? Things change, sometimes things go bad, often they improve. Fortunately these days it's easy to update books! If you want to get those updates for FREE, including any new versions of this book that I publish, please go to my webiste and sign-up.

http://NonBoringTravelGuides.com/PackingBonus

Practical Safe Travel Tips and Travel Health Advice

Planning on travelling but worried about getting sick? Or maybe you're happy to travel but your parents are convinced that you will end up robbed, raped, and left bleeding in a ditch and suffering from malaria?

So you want foolproof safe travel solutions? Sorry, the world does not come with guarantees - and the author is not offering any. Instead, blending humour and experience, she tries to separate the sensational news headlines from the reality of travel.

This is a not a thick book, it's a concise guide which addresses how to avoid dying out there, interspersed with stories from the author's own experience. The author hasn't died yet, so her advice must be worth something.

Why You Shouldn't Buy This Book

Will this book replace your doctor's advice? Nope. Is it useful for a high-profile exec worried about the threat of kidnap? Ahhh, no. Will it entertain and inform the average inexperienced traveller? That's the aim!

This book won't give you all the answers, and your parents will probably still worry. But its a start for anyone looking for safe travel tips and travel health advice.

Yup this is a Non-Boring Travel Guide. If you don't have a sense of humour, I suggest you might just want to skip right on by. This is written by a traveller not a medical professional, or even an ex-Special Services member. I'm just a gal, who travels ... a lot. After 30 years I've come down with the odd disease while travelling, and faced death on several occasions, but, to date, I've survived. Must be doing something right.

The Non-Boring Safe Travel Guide even has some useful information:

- *why visiting your favourite medical professional before you leave home can be a great investment;*

- *mosquitoes, and why you should learn to hate them;*

- the number one cause of death of American tourists overseas: hint, its not a disease;

- surviving local transport;

- how to avoid being a thief magnet on the street;

- fool-proof way to avoid having your valuables stolen overseas.

The world is really a much, much safer place than the local news media would have you believe. This realistic guide is designed to inform and encourage you to get out there and really enjoy it.

For more details including where to buy please check out:

www.NonBoringTravelGuides.com

31259569R00065

Made in the USA
San Bernardino, CA
05 March 2016